The Quick & Easy Guide to ICEBREAKERS & TEAMBUILDERS

Jon Tucker

Author of The Ultimate Icebreaker & Teambuilder Guide

jont007@yahoo.com

Lulu.com Publishing

ISBN 978-1-105-92895-6

FROM THE AUTHOR

As society moves more and more into a technological age, the importance of face-to-face interactions becomes more crucial. Icebreakers and teambuilders are valuable now more than ever. Whereas people may have chatted on the phone before meeting in person, it is more likely that facebook, texting or other social media start before the introductions are made.

I love technology and have incorporated a few technological icebreakers into this guide to use these resources. My hope is that you will find this guide to be handy and portable for many different occasions!

This book is dedicated to the students I have worked with who provide me with energy, enthusiasm and motivation. In keeping with this support, a portion of the proceeds of the sales of this book go towards scholarships to help make higher education accessible to them.

Enjoy the activities and the book!

Jon Tucker

Also by Jon Tucker...

The Ultimate Icebreaker & Teambuilder Guide
© 2007 by Western Oregon University
Lulu.com Publishing (available everywhere)
ISBN 978-1-4303-0693-1

Over 200 activities and exercises in full detail! Searchable index and facilitation questions – good for all groups! The 2nd edition will be coming soon!

TABLE OF CONTENTS

WELCOME!

This guide is for you! This icebreaker and teambuilder guide will provide you with examples, tools, resources and 69 different activities with 174 variations of activities to keep things hopping!

In addition, the guide is organized in a way that can give you what you need for "name games"; provide spur-of-the-moment energetic icebreakers; and give you some meaningful ideas for developing groups into teams!

It is also organized so that you can adapt activities in multiple ways! This can give you even more variations of activities to keep things fresh – even for people who might say, "Oh, I've done that icebreaker a thousand times!"

Lastly, the book is arranged so that a minimal amount of materials is required. We know that sometimes materials for activities can be hard to find (especially if you are in a hurry), but the ones in this book are easy and can be found at your local grocery store, office, residence hall room, apartment. Many don't require anything at all!

Best of luck and enjoy the fun and excitement that these activities can provide!

FACILITATING ICEBREAKERS & TEAMBUILDERS

When conducting any sort of icebreaker or teambuilder training, it is imperative that the facilitator be prepared for the activity and have a fair idea of what will happen with their group. Some considerations may be: age/maturity of the group, size of the group, familiarity of participants with each other, how "touchy-feely" is the group, etc. This next section will talk about tools and methods for successful facilitators.

Facilitation Philosophy

Successful facilitators will walk into each activity and see it as an opportunity to achieve an objective or two with group learning and development. One of the primary purposes of doing an activity is to encourage groups to either develop and grow, or reach some understanding about a specific topic area. As long as the facilitator goes into the exercise with the mindset that "our group is going to accomplish something," the participants themselves will be more invested in what is going on. An activity without a purpose may be viewed as a waste of time (theirs and yours!)

Prior to any activity presented in this or other guides, the facilitator should be able to answer the following questions:

- What is the purpose of this activity?
- What will this activity provide for the group?
- Does this group of participants need or want these objectives?
- Do I have the materials necessary?
- Is the group at the appropriate place for the level of risk for the activity?
- Is there an adequate space or facility for this activity?
- Do I have enough time for the activity and the important facilitation that will follow?
- Am I prepared to adapt the activity for time constraints or for accommodating people with disabilities?

Only when you, as a facilitator, can comfortably answer these questions are you ready to present the activity for the group. You must know the group well enough to be able to set up an activity. There have been too many times when an activity was planned that the group wasn't prepared for!

Note, however, that it is perfectly appropriate for the objective to be "I want people to get to know each other better." For many icebreakers, the ability to facilitate comfort with each other, understand names, build trust or further develop relationships are key objectives.

Facilitation Questions

Facilitation takes place after the activity is complete, yet should still be fresh in the participant's minds. Some of the best facilitation questions may ask participants to determine what they saw, what they thought and what they felt. (Seeing, Thinking and Feeling) These three areas are similar, but get at different learning styles. What a participant saw may or may not be congruent with thoughts and feelings.

Facilitation questions are designed to provide for engagement and participant learning. When developing your own questions, ask yourself:

- What kind of answer do I expect from this question?
- Will I get honest answers?
- Will this question address an area of learning that the activity focuses on? For example, if the activity addresses communication issues, will the question hit on this area?
- Is the question at a depth that is appropriate for how well the group knows each other? For example, you wouldn't ask people to share some important personal secret if they have just met ten minutes ago.

Here are some other generic facilitation questions that would work for almost any activity:

- What was challenging about this activity?
- How did people interact and communicate during this exercise?
- What were your initial impressions of this activity?
- How does this activity relate to this group and the future?
- What surprised you while you were doing this activity?

I would encourage facilitators to follow up and keep the lessons of these activities in mind for future learning. It is always effective later on in training or in a group to say, "Remember when we did the __________ activity? How does this relate to...?"

Many participants will expect something tangible to come out of an activity. Some will want to know how it relates to "real life" situations. As a facilitator, think about this issue and discuss it with group organizers or participants themselves. Tailor your facilitation questions to specific topics within a group. If a group has been dealing with issues of conflict lately, then address facilitation questions to this area. A teambuilding activity can only build a team successfully if it addresses issues found within the team!

Facilitation Challenges

Leading an activity can be difficult if you are faced with people that are uninterested in the activity or being involved with the group. When you are faced with resistance or hesitancy, there are a few ways you can approach the issue:

- Address the concerns directly. Ask the group why they are hesitant to participate in the activity. As a facilitator, encourage a realistic dialogue about the issues and concerns to engage the group into participating.
- Discuss varied learning styles. Every person learns differently so you must engage people in visual, auditory and kinesthetic learning opportunities. Ask that everyone participate so that learning and the experience can be equal to everyone in the group.
- Leave the decision of whether to do the activity up to the group. You might wish to postpone the activity until the energy level or group is ready for the exercise. As a facilitator, have a back-up plan in case problems arise with any activity.

As a facilitator, you will find that some of these activities fit well with your style and others will not. I recommend that you match those you like with those that you feel are most effective!

CONSIDERATIONS FOR PEOPLE WITH DISABILITIES

The exercises here have been designed so that most people in our society will be able to participate with or without accommodations. Some may require some thought in the event that not everyone is TAB (Temporarily Able-Bodied – the idea that anyone can receive a disability at any point in time in their lives).

Here are some thoughts to consider with these activities:

- Don't assume that someone with a disability will be unable to participate.
- Explain the activity to people and simply ask if there are any concerns or challenges anyone might have to the activity. People can respond privately if they wish. Ask any group leaders familiar with the participants if there are any potential changes that need to be made.
- If you have questions about a person's participation in an activity, ask them how they would like to engage in the exercise. They might suggest a change that enables everyone to participate fully.

- If an activity requires quick movement and someone is mobility-impaired, an option might be to explain that people who can walk or run can only walk heel-to-toe.
- If an activity requires throwing, ask people to pass objects instead.
- Examine activities for visual impairment or hearing impairment. As a facilitator, how will you adapt an exercise prior to its beginning?

Remember to have some flexibility and foresight with any of these activities to do what they are meant to do – build inclusion and create a team!

Take the couple of minutes to consider these questions when working with an unseen group and have a couple back-up plans! Make sure you examine the room prior to starting any activity.

Also, keep in mind that not all disabilities are readily visible to you as a facilitator! Word games or similar activities may pose a challenge for someone with a cognitive or learning disability!

QUICK! I NEED A...

This section is going to provide you with exactly what you need on a moment's notice! No or minimal resources are needed and are divided into categories and page numbers so that you can instantly find some of the "favorites".

So, do you need an activity that is...??

Silly

Low-Key

Be sure to read through the various activities because you may have other favorites than the ones listed here!

NAME GAMES

Name games are imperative for new groups, particularly if they are going to be working together repeatedly over time. Some people are better at names than others, so these activities provide repetition and mnemonics to assist with this ask.

Remember to get everyone involved and examine all activities to make sure they are inclusive and appropriate for your group.

Acronym Adventures

Time Required: 5-14 minutes
Materials Needed: None
Activity Level: Low
Number of Participants: 8-40

All participants should each form a circle or, alternatively, this activity can be done in smaller groups if the total number of participants is larger. Each person should take a few minutes to think of things that describe themselves using one adjective starting with each letter of their first name. For example, Jon could be: Jocular, Ostentatious and Noisy. Each person will need to go around, state their name and give the acronym adjectives that make their name.

Variations:

- Ask people to remember the names of the people who have gone before them.
- No one in the entire group can use the same adjective. Once it is used, each person must find another one.
- Ask the group to select the adjectives for that participant and that person whose name it is can give a yes or no as to whether that word fits or not. Discussion on first impressions can then ensue.

Adjective Name Game

Time Required: 10-20 minutes
Materials Needed: None
Activity Level: Low
Number of Participants: 10-24

This is a simple name game where you gather the participants in a circle (square, octagon or other shape). As a facilitator, start off introducing yourself by using an adjective or other word that describes yourself and then state your name.

"Jovial Jon" for example. The next person then would state the first person's adjective and name and then their own adjective & name combination. This continues until everyone has gone around and finished.

Variations:

- Go out of order. Make it a random mix or go alphabetically.
- People can move around the circle when the facilitator yells, "Switch!" (or three participants all agree).
- Ask for two adjectives per person.
- Don't require everyone to state the names of the people before them.
- Use an adverb and adjective like "Extremely excellent Erica" or "Deliciously devious Dan" to keep all in the same letter.

Ask Me a Question

Time Required: 6-15 minutes
Materials Needed: None
Activity Level: Low
Number of Participants: 6-18

People form circles where everyone can see each other. The activity is very simple – the facilitator will take a question (or more) and ask each participant to go around and answer that question. You may also use something from "The Book of Questions" or similar reading. Some questions could include:

- Where would you go if you could take a vacation and money was no object?
- When you were a child, what did you want to be growing up?
- Who did you idolize growing up?
- Who motivates or inspires you?
- What is the last book you read?
- What the world could do without is…
- What would be your first reaction if aliens landed outside right now and why?
- What is one regret that you hold with your life so far?
- What age in your life did you find to be most fulfilling and what age were you happy to move beyond?

Variations:

- Ask participants to generate questions themselves for the group.

Blanket Name Game

Time Required: 6-15 minutes
Materials Needed: Large blanket
Activity Level: Low
Number of Participants: 8-30

Participants should divide themselves into two equal groups. Each group should sit together on their own side of the room facing other members of the group. Have two neutral volunteers (or facilitators) hold up a blanket between the two groups so they cannot see each other. Once ready, one member of each group should move quietly up to their side of the blanket and face the blanket without touching it. When ready, the facilitators should drop the blanket and each person at the blanket should try to say the name of the person on the other side. Whoever says the other person's name first, wins. Whoever loses joins the winning team. The game continues until people are satisfied. Note: watch for reflected surfaces when playing (no cheating!)

Variations:

- Participants can put more than one person up.
- People must face different directions.
- You may have people write the names on paper or pick up a laminated card from among a collection of everyone's names.

Charades Introductions

Time Required: 10-30 minutes
Materials Needed: None
Activity Level: Medium
Number of Participants: 4-18

This activity works well for brand new groups. Ask each person to spend a couple minutes thinking about three items, characteristics, objects or actions that represent themselves. Once everyone is ready, they will introduce themselves in front of the rest of the group and will use charades to try to convey each of those three pieces. Once someone from the group has figured out what that piece is, they should say it out loud and the person can then move on to the next item. The activity continues until everyone has gone.

Variations:

- Use nametags to help facilitate name recognition.
- Use a theme to help people determine what those three items or characteristics may be (childhood, sports, entertainment, family, etc.)
- Instill a time limit for each item. If it isn't guessed within 15 seconds, then move on.
- Make it a competition for presenters to have everyone guess their three things in the fewest cumulative seconds of time.

Group Juggle

Time Required: 10-25 minutes
Materials Needed: Balls or other soft objects (rolled socks work too)
Activity Level: Low
Number of Participants: 10-35

The group should start in a circle a little more than shoulder-width apart, facing the middle. The leader should start with an object in their hand (something soft - a tennis ball, beanbag or even roll of toilet paper!) The leader will state their name, say another person's name from the group, and then gently toss the object to that group member. That group member will reply, "Thank you <leader's name>". That person will then repeat their own name, say another's name and toss the item to that person, and so on, continuing the cycle. Once everyone has had a chance to toss the item the last person left should toss the item back to the starting person.

It helps during the first round to have everyone that has already tossed the object to cross their arms to prevent repetition. After the first time through, explain that everyone will continue that same pattern, but add more and more objects so that there may be several objects being tossed simultaneously, all keeping that same pattern. Remember to keep the names and introductions going! That is the point of the activity, after all!

Variations:

- If an object is dropped, you may elect to have the activity start all over again with the starting person to make the activity more challenging.
- Mix up the sizes and types of objects being tossed (safe things only!)
- Facilitators can quiz everyone on names afterwards.
- Two different types of items require two different directions. One starts one way and then other goes the opposite direction.

How Am I Unique?

Time Required: 10-20 minutes
Materials Needed: None
Activity Level: Low
Number of Participants: 10-35

Gather all of the participants into a circle. Starting with the facilitator or a volunteer, each person does an introduction and describes one thing that they think is unique about them or some interesting fact that they believe no one else has. If someone else in the group has shared that experience, they raise their hand. If that is the case, then the person speaking has to come up with something else until a unique item is named. Go around until everyone has had a chance to be introduced.

Variations:

- If there are people who also have that same "unique" thing about themselves, the volunteer must remember those people's names and say them out loud. At the end, they will be required to remember those names.
- For smaller groups, you can ask people to list two things that are unique.

Introduction Interview

Time Required: 8-25 minutes
Materials Needed: None
Activity Level: Low
Number of Participants: 8-30

Ask participants to pair up with someone that they do not know. Explain that for two minutes, each person will need to talk to their partner (without stopping and for the entire two minutes) about themselves. Topics could include high school, family, hobbies, academic areas, memorably moments, etc. It is often advantageous to write possible topics down somewhere for people to view. This may be difficult for some people and easier for others. When done, the roles should then switch for another two minutes. When completed, each person in the pair (if time and group size allow) should introduce and provide a brief summary about their partner to the rest of the group using the information gathered in the interview. If the group size prohibits everyone from sharing, put the pairs into groups of 6 or 8 or so and then conduct the interviews in those larger groups.

Variations:

- This exercise can be done so that the listener is told to provide no body language or non-verbal feedback. This can be done in conjunction with a discussion about the importance of feedback and two-way communication.

- Introduce a theme for the relaying of information. Perhaps the interview has to be done like a news magazine, like an MTV or entertainment show, like a political debate, a cartoon, or other idea.
- You may also adapt and edit the amount of time for the interview depending upon the size of the group, but more than 2 minutes can be much more challenging.

Motion Name Game

Time Required: 6-30 minutes
Materials Needed: None
Activity Level: Medium
Number of Participants: 8-30

The group should start of in a circle, facing inwards about arm's length apart. This exercise is similar to the Adjective Name Game except that instead of inventing an adjective with a name, each person will repeat their name and create some motion or quick action that represents them in some way. Someone can do a somersault, wave to the group or make some other individualized motion. The next person in the group must then repeat that person's name and activity and then do their own. This repeats until the entire circle has gone. The last person will then have done everyone's name and motion before doing their own!

Variations:

- For small enough groups, motions can only use a single body part and no one may duplicate.
- Participants must link hands and the motions should connect to form a "wave."
- Participants may go in an order that isn't in the circle (alphabetically, etc.)

My Story

Time Required: 15-30 minutes
Materials Needed: None
Activity Level: Low
Number of Participants: 10-25

Form participants in a circle, preferably in a comfortable position. This exercise requires everyone to introduce themselves and tell a story about some aspect or piece of history in their life. Stories should be about 30 seconds - 2 minutes in length depending upon the size of the group. One requirement is that the person says their name at least 5 times during the course of the storytelling (speaking in the third person works well). Everyone will be required to participate and quality or excitement level of the story doesn't matter. It should simply be a story to get to know each other.

Variations:

- You can tailor this exercise to be more specific. You can have themes based upon sports, childhood stories, getting in trouble, cooking, embarrassing moments or more.
- For a particularly dynamic group, you can encourage people to tell their story and act out parts with movement, sound effects and more.

My Three Descriptors

Time Required: 8-30 minutes
Materials Needed: Markers & Nametags
Activity Level: Low
Number of Participants: 4-40

This activity is good to start a group off at the very beginning of a training or orientation. Distribute markers to participants and give each person a blank nametag. Everyone should then be asked to print their name in big letters on the top part of their nametag and then asked to draw three things on their nametag that represents who they are on the bottom portion of the tag. After everyone has completed drawing, participants should be asked to go around the group and share their names, what they drew on the tag, and why it is important to them.

Variations:

- Use themes for the three things on the nametags (childhood, sports, entertainment, family, friends, school, etc.)
- Get people in pairs to share more in-depth about what those three things mean. After a minute or two, switch partners.

Name Toss

Time Required: 6-12 minutes
Materials Needed: One ball or soft object
Activity Level: Low
Number of Participants: 15-45

Arrange participants in a circle with everyone facing the middle. The facilitator should have a ball or other soft object. Before tossing the ball, say the name of the person you are throwing to. After you throw, cross arms. After everyone has received the ball and is sitting, surprise them by making them go in the exact opposite order and remember the name of the person who threw the ball to them.

Variations:

- Not only do people go in the opposite order, switch up everyone's locations in the circle.
- Ask people to say the name of the person they received the ball from AND the one they are giving it to.
- Have the circle slowly rotate as the exercise takes place.
- Create "penalties" or other questions if the ball is dropped by anyone. (Share their favorite animal, embarrassing moment, etc.)

Shoe Game

Time Required: 10-25 minutes
Materials Needed: None
Activity Level: Low
Number of Participants: 8-40

The group should be in a circle, close to one another facing the middle. Everyone should remove their shoes, tie the two shoes together (or somehow secure them), and place them randomly in a large pile in the middle of the group. If the shoes don't tie, then keep them together as best as possible. Have a volunteer go to the pile of shoes, pick a pair (not their own) and return to the circle. That person should then make one statement about the owner of the shoes that they picked. (i.e. "The owner of these shoes must want to be comfortable because of the padding and soft leather!" The owner of the shoes then will come forward, introduce themselves and pick out another pair of shoes to introduce. This goes until everyone has had a chance to participate!

Variations:

- Participants must tell a 30-second story about the shoes or a continuing story from one person to the next.
- Have the person who drew the shoes take the shoes to the person who they believe to be the owner.

Speed Friends

Time Required: 30-50 minutes
Materials Needed: None (question lists, nametags optional)
Activity Level: Low
Number of Participants: 10-40

Break participants into two subgroups and ask the first group to sit in a circle facing outwards. The second group should sit in a larger circle, partnered with someone on the inner circle, facing inwards (towards each other). Each pairing will have a set amount of time (2-3 minutes depending upon the size of the group) to have a "speed date." In this case, a "date" is simply a chance to meet a new friend! People should exchange their names and talk about themselves during the exercise with an ideal being a balance between both people sharing and listening. After that set amount of time, the facilitator will require one of the circles to rotate to the next person and the time begins again. You can prepare a series of questions to start the conversations available for the participants or you can announce a topic at each rotation. Remember, everyone should be sharing their name as well!

Variations:

- People can take notes about the individuals they meet.
- Randomly switch the directions of lines so it is more unpredictable!

Tall Tales

Time Required: 10-25 minutes
Materials Needed: None
Activity Level: Low
Number of Participants: 10-24

This activity builds levity for a group, especially if they are going to be one that will work together for a period of time. This name game requires that each person think up an introduction/story about one of the other people there! People should form a circle and everyone needs to take a minute to think of a story about the person to their left. After everyone is ready, the first person introduces themselves and turns to introduce the person next to them. The person will make up a story about that person - often the more ridiculous, the better. It should be something that is light and untrue. The game continues with the person who just was described now will introduce themselves and the person next to them and then state their story. The activity continues until everyone has gone.

An example might be:
"You may not know this, but Angela has been scuba diving on three different continents. Not only has she swum with sharks, but she has captured two in cages and keeps them as pets in her aquarium at home. She prefers to feed them live kittens, but usually gets by with rats and Twinkies. This is Angela!"

Variations:

- Go out of order.
- Ask people to draw names out of a hat to determine who describes whom.
- Ask for people to get with their person and do a two-minute introduction overview. Switch so the other partner can do the interview. Use this information as the basis for the story, so that there is some basis in fact.
- Incorporate body movement into the activity for extra dynamics.
- Instead of verbal pieces, the stories must be pantomimed and performed.

Whomp'Em

Time Required: 6-12 minutes
Materials Needed: Sponge bat, Styrofoam or rolled up newspaper
Activity Level: Medium
Number of Participants: 10-30

The group is asked to sit in a circle about an arm's length apart with everyone's legs extended straight in front of them. There should be enough room for an opening in the center so that the "Whomp'Em Master" has room to move around a little. The Whomp'Em Master will use the Whomp'Em sword in the game. Someone starts the round by saying the name of a member of the group.

The Master must Whomp (hit) the shoes/feet/legs of that person before that person can say another person's name. They cannot repeat a name that has been said in that round already. When the Master succeeds in Whomping someone before they say someone else's name, that person becomes the new Master. You may also set a rule that if anyone flinches or moves their legs away, they automatically become the Whomp'Em Master in the middle.

Variations:

- After a second time in the middle, that middle person must do a little song or dance for the group.

- Instead of hitting the legs of people, the person in the middle must hit between the feet of that person.
- Whomp'Em Masters must say one or two things about themselves whenever they go into the middle.

ICEBREAKERS

Icebreakers are those activities meant to energize a group. They typically focus on trust-building, energy levels, group dynamics and such. They can be extremely energetic or more sedentary depending upon the needs of the group.

Most of the time, there is no direct educational message with the activities...they are meant to build connections within the group. You certainly could create questions if you wish focusing on the thoughts and feelings that the exercises generated.

Feel free to use all of the variations, or think of your own, in order to tailor the icebreaker to the needs of your group!

Amoeba Tag

Time Required: 10-20 minutes
Materials Needed: None – optional cones to mark boundaries
Activity Level: High
Number of Participants: 8-50

Establish boundaries for the game so that there is a large enough space for everyone to move around. One person should volunteer or be selected to be "it." For the purposes of the game, it is good to have someone that is pretty quick to start the activity. Here is the background to relay to the participants: The person chosen is now a single-celled organism that has a strong desire to grow and expand. That person will chase the other participants and if they tag someone, they then join hands and collectively, the two-person team is the "amoeba" and is "it." If either person touches someone, that next person joins the amoeba. This continues as the amoeba tags additional people until eventually the amoeba has all but one person, who is the winner.

Variations:

- If there is a large number of participants, you may designate two or more people as "it" to start.
- One large amoeba may also be subdivided into smaller ones if some situation occurs: time passes, etc.

Back To Back

Time Required: 5-15 minutes
Materials Needed: None
Activity Level: High
Number of Participants: 8-300

Every group member should find a partner of approximately equal height and weight. The partners will start by standing back-to-back and locking arms behind them with their partner. With arms locked at all times and starting from a standing position, the partners should attempt to sit down, kick their legs out and have their bottoms sitting on the ground. Once that is completed by everyone, the facilitator will encourage people to try to stand back up.

Once people have completed that task, get people into groups of four, lock arms and attempt the same task. This can be done by combining groups into eight, sixteen or even more! This activity works well to begin a series on trust building or as an energizer. With this activity, please keep in mind the surface of the floor in case of "hard landings!"

Variations:

- Once participants are in groups of four or more, play some music and encourage groups to dance.
- While linked, you could create a "tag" game with the groups.

Barnyard Animals

Time Required: 6-15 minutes
Materials Needed: None
Activity Level: Medium
Number of Participants: 15-300

Ask participants of the group to silently think of some barnyard animal that they will wish to become for this activity. You can alternatively give people the option of choosing from a few of the following: cat, dog, cow, chicken, sheep, horse, duck, goat, goose, llama, pig or other animal. When you tell them to begin, each person will close their eyes and find all the members of the group that have the same animal, using only the animal's own noises as a guide. Once everyone finds all of their own animals, they can open their eyes. The facilitator (and/or a couple of volunteers) should try to be a "spotter" during the activity by making sure people don't get way off line or walk into walls. Participants should cross their hands in front of their chests as "bumpers" in case of collision. Keep in mind safety and no one should be moving too fast.

Variations:

- You can also use this exercise with "Sea World Sounds" such as dolphins, whales, jellyfish or other sea creatures that may or may not have recognizable sounds.
- Do dinosaur sounds and provide examples to the group.

Birdie on a Perch

Time Required: 8-20 minutes
Materials Needed: None
Activity Level: High
Number of Participants: 15-80

This is a very physical activity that involves a lot of contact! First, ask for participants to find a partner. Everyone will need to form two circles, one person on the inner circle and one on the outer circle. The inner circle should stand about an arm's width apart and face left. The outer circle should be about four feet away and facing the opposite direction as the inner circle. Once the activity begins, each circle will rotate in different directions. When the facilitator says, "Birdie on a Perch," each member of the pair must find each other and hop on the other person's back (like a piggyback). The last pair to do this successfully is out of that round and should sit on the sidelines. The game continues until only one pair remains. Remember, this is a physical activity and talk to participants about safety being the #1 priority here!

Variations:

- Instead of piggyback, participants must link arms with partners behind their backs.
- Add some music to the activity.
- Do it in sets of three – one on back, one on hands and knees between middle person's legs.

Body English

Time Required: 5-10 minutes
Materials Needed: None
Activity Level: Medium
Number of Participants: 6-120

The object of this exercise is for small groups of participants to use their bodies to clearly spell words out to the other groups. Divide participants into subgroups and ask them to get together to plan and spell out a word (from a list that you can provide or make up) using only their bodies. Everyone must participate in the activity, which can be challenging for large groups trying to make very small words. Groups must create the word silently for extra challenge. The other group(s) must figure out what they are spelling. Start with single words or maybe move to phrases as the groups get better at spelling in this fashion. The size of the words depends upon the size of the subgroups.

Variations:

- Groups can buzz in as a competition to guess the words being created earning points.
- Phrases would be simple 3-5 word combinations. Once the first word is done, the group immediately moves to the next word. Groups may guess word-by-word or wait until the entire phrase is complete.

Catch Me If You Can

Time Required: 4-10 minutes
Materials Needed: None
Activity Level: Low
Number of Participants: 6-200

Players should be paired up and divided into two lines facing each other. Participants should be given about 30 seconds to look at their partners and take in all the details of that individual. The leader then instructs the two lines to turn away from the center and not look at their partners. One or both lines (facilitator's choice) has another 15-30 seconds to change something about their appearance (change watch to a different arm, unbutton a button, remove a belt, etc.) The change should be discrete, but visible to the partner. The players are then to turn to face each other and have up to 30 seconds to discover the physical changes that have been made. You can do this activity a few different times, giving participants time to think of what changes they could make.

Variations:

- One person goes at a time, leaves the room and makes the changes, perhaps for the entire group.
- Changes can occur during breaks in a training or other program, reconvening afterwards.

Charlie's Angels

Time Required: 15-25 minutes
Materials Needed: None
Activity Level: Low
Number of Participants: 12-45

All participants will need to form a circle facing the center about three feet apart from their neighbors. The facilitator becomes "Charlie" and will start off the game. Each participant will need to learn the motions of this game, so the leader should be very familiar with the activity. It works best if there are another three people that know the formations as well to demonstrate to the group. If not, then the facilitator can show them.

In this game, Charlie will point to someone in the circle of participants. Charlie will then count to eight (or other number) as quickly or slowly as they would like (although slower is better while people are learning the game.) The person pointed to, and the people on their immediate left and right have to complete the motion before Charlie counts to eight. If any one of the people is slow, does the wrong motion or doesn't move at all, they are now the person in the middle. In the event that more than one person does something incorrectly or slow, the person originally pointed to defaults to become Charlie. The following are the motions that can be used in this activity:

- "Fire Hydrant" – the person in the middle stands with hands together, raised in the air above their head, while the people on either side must turn and "lift their legs" towards the person in the middle.
- "Charlie's Angels" – the person in the middle must stand with their hands in a gun motion and pointing in the air. The people on either side need to turn away from the center person and make the same gun motions. Facial expressions are appreciated!
- "Elephant" – the person in the middle must take one hand and grab the ear on the opposite side of their head. They must then stick the other hand out like an elephant's trunk. The people on either side must make their arms into a giant "C" to simulate big ears on the person in the middle.
- "Mosquito" – the person in the middle must put their hand (palm inward) up to their nose and stick the index finger of the other hand through the fingers to simulate a mosquito's nose. The people on the sides must turn away from the center person and simulate flapping wings quickly with their hands.
- "Alligator" – the person in the middle must make both of their arms move in a chomping mouth motion. The people on the sides must move behind the middle person, forming a train as the

"tail" behind the center person, wiggling their behinds.

- "Flight Attendant" – the person in the middle must simulate putting on the oxygen mask (as in an airplane's safety procedures) while people on the sides must simulate pointing out the emergency exit doors on an airplane.
- "Chia Pet" – the person in the middle must get on their hands and knees while the people on either side must put their hands in the center person's hair and with those hands, make a motion as if the hair was growing while saying "Cha Cha Cha Chia".
- "Luau" – the person in the middle must get on their hands and knees and mimic having a large apple in their mouth while the persons on either side must make hula motions with their bodies.
- "Cow" – the person in the middle extends their arms in front of them and points their thumbs down. The people on the sides must grab a thumb and make cow milking motions.
- "Hear No Evil" – the person in the middle must make a motion by covering eyes, the person on the middle's right must cover their ears and the person on the left side must cover their mouth. The appearance should appear as a "Hear no evil, see no evil, and speak no evil" from an observer's point of view.

Feel free to make up other motions that you feel work well, but remember that the activity becomes significantly more difficult with the more formations you create.

Variations:

- Vary the amount of time groups have to get the motions correct.
- Instead of pointing to the middle, Charlie moves between two people and becomes the middle. The last of the two to do the motion becomes Charlie.
- Encourage participants to make up a new motion and formation halfway through the activity, which you then have participants vote upon. The winning vote or two will be incorporated into your game.

Color, Car, Character

Time Required: 12-30 minutes
Materials Needed: None
Activity Level: Low
Number of Participants: 10-40

Ask participants to form a circle. Participants will have a couple of minutes to think about a type of car, a color and a fictional character that best describes their personality. After selecting, each person should give a brief explanation as to why they chose those particular items. The activity continues until everyone has shared.

Variations:

- Ask participants to verbally describe the significance of their choices.
- Add additional "C's" to the activity: Cereal, Clothes, Candy, Card Game, etc.
- Provide themes to the fictional characters – from movies, TV, cartoons, etc.

Detective

Time Required: 8-15 minutes
Materials Needed: None
Activity Level: Low
Number of Participants: 12-50

This is a game of "Hide and Seek" but done in the open! Before the actual game begins, have everyone circulate around the room in any direction. Explain to the participants, "Whenever you see an empty space open up in the room, you should move quickly to try and fill in that empty space. As other spaces open up, you then move to fill those, etc." Everyone should be moving silently.

After a few minutes of walking around, give instructions to the participants, "You are detectives. Select someone in the room to observe, but don't let them know who it is. As you walk around the room, make sure that you keep that person in sight at all times, but do not let that person know you are watching them! Don't be obvious!" Let everyone wander around and shadow each other for a few minutes and remind people not to talk. It may be good for participants to make it difficult to be seen by hiding in and out of others in the group. Players have to remember to keep looking at the person they are observing. Remind players that because they are self-selecting people to watch that not everyone playing may have someone watching them and others may have more than one!

There are two ways to end the activity. You can ask participants to "Follow your person around no matter where they go." Players may eventually form into some sort of pattern. You may also ask them after awhile if they correctly identified their detectives! Alternatively, you can ask players to stop and guess out loud who is watching them!

Variations:

- Limit the amount of time to determine who is following them.
- At some point in the activity, the person must try to gently touch the person they are following, without that person knowing it.
- Select one person (secretly) who isn't watching anyone to leave the confines of a single room and adventure out to create some more intrigue!

Do You Love Your Neighbor?

<u>*Time Required:*</u> 10-20 minutes
<u>*Materials Needed:*</u> None
<u>*Activity Level:*</u> Medium
<u>*Number of Participants:*</u> 14-80

Ask participants to form a circle, standing about two feet apart from each other, facing the middle. Everyone should remove their shoes and place them immediately behind them in the circle to mark their location. One person will begin play in the middle of the circle, removing their shoes from the circle so that there is one less set of shoes than people playing.

The middle person can then say to someone in the outer circle, "<person's name>, do you love your neighbor?" The individual pointed out should say, "Yes, I love my neighbors <left person> and <right person>, but I REALLY love people that <name some trait - are wearing green, are from Oregon, have been out of the country, etc.> This trait MUST be something that is true for the middle person!

At that point all members of the group who fit that characteristic must move and find a new spot in the circle at least three spaces away from where they were standing. The person with no space (last person remaining) becomes the caller in the middle. When asked if they love their neighbors, the person pointed to can also say, "No, I don't" in which case the two "neighbors" on either side of them must switch places with one another, and the last person to their space becomes the caller.

Variations:

- Add penalties for being in the middle three, four, five or more times. This person may have to sing, dance or do something a little embarrassing in front of the group (harmless fun!)
- If someone says, "No, I don't [love my neighbor]", everyone playing must switch places.
- The activity can be done with fewer introductions, by merely having the person in the middle dictate the terms of play. The middle person would introduce themselves and say, "My name is Jon and I want to meet someone who likes to go camping." At that point, everyone who likes camping would switch places with the middle person joining the circle.

Elbow Tag

Time Required: 8-25 minutes
Materials Needed: None (Optional cones to mark boundaries)
Activity Level: High
Number of Participants: 14-36

Ask participants to find a partner and link arms at the elbows, facing the same direction. The pairs should spread out around the designated playing area and two individuals should be chosen to be "it". One is the chaser and one is to be chased. Once the game begins, the person being chased will run around the area to some other pair of people and hook elbows with another person (facing either direction). The third person in the group on the far side of the trio is now the one being chased and should run off. The chaser must then chase after this new player. If at any time chaser tags the person being chased, the person that was being chased spins around three times and becomes the new chaser. The original chaser is now the one being chased. The game continues until completed, but you may want to have a time limit to prevent overly tired chasers and to allow continued participation from the group. Also note that people should be careful running as well as violent arm linking at a full sprint for safety reasons.

Variations:

- With large numbers of people, have more than one chaser and chase-ee combinations.
- Instead of joining arms, participants should have hands out in "high five" positions. Once someone is "high fived," then the third person in that group is being chased. This eliminates some potential violent jerking from overly-enthusiastic participants.

Evolution

Time Required: 10-20 minutes
Materials Needed: None
Activity Level: Low
Number of Participants: 16-50

The facilitator should choose an "Evolver" before the game begins. Explain to the participants that the Evolver can change people into animals simply by whispering to them. Everyone else is allowed to communicate as well, but only in a whisper. Ask people to mill about as if at a party. Encourage people to shake hands and whisper to others in the group. At some point, the Evolver says quietly to another player, "You are a turtle (cow, duck, bird, hippopotamus, other animal.)" The player whispered to must count to ten seconds silently to themselves and then slowly turn into that animal (over the next 15 seconds or so). No other player is allowed to use the phrase, "You're a..." except the Evolver.

Gradually players will turn into the various animals. If any non-animal player thinks that they know the identity of the "Evolver," then they should raise their hand and yell, "I accuse!" Everyone freezes in place at that point and the player points to the person that they think is the Evolver and says, "You are the Evolver!" If correct, then a new Evolver is chosen, but if the accusation is incorrect, the accuser becomes a pre-set animal (Ducks are good) and the game continues. When in animal form, players should be able to talk but use a cow-like (or their appropriate animal) "accents." They must walk like that animal, etc. The activity continues until a set period of time or a few rounds have taken place.

Variations:

- Successful accusers of the Evolver can receive some little prize or bonus.
- Use different themes, other than animals. People revert to children, amoebas or other ideas.
- Evolvers instead of whispering will wink at someone. The person winked at will become some pre-designated animal (dinosaur, etc.)

Flashlight Tag

<u>*Time Required:*</u> 10-20 minutes
<u>*Materials Needed:*</u> Flashlights
<u>*Activity Level:*</u> Medium
<u>*Number of Participants:*</u> 6-20

This game is played in the dark – either outside or a large interior space with lots of furniture and other areas to hide. As a facilitator, you should define a clear playing area. One person is "it" and will get a couple seconds of flashlight time in the eyes to create some night vision imparity for a little while. The objective is for the chaser to find and "tag" another person with their flashlight. The person who was tagged should then announce loudly that they have been tagged. The original chaser then gets a 15-second head start, the new chaser must do the flashlight impairment and then the game continues.

<u>Variations:</u>

- Use camera flashes instead of flashlights. The cameras can be actual photographs to verify someone was tagged. Otherwise, the honor system is in place to verify someone has been "tagged."
- Use different color light filters on flashlights or add strobe lights to areas to create confusion.
- Tagged people, instead of becoming the "chaser" must be frozen in place until everyone is found and tagged.

Follow the Leader

Time Required: 10-18 minutes
Materials Needed: None
Activity Level: High
Number of Participants: 10-50

This is the standard children's game that actually works well with any energetic group! Assign or ask for a volunteer to lead the group. That person should walk and go over, around, and under things in the general area (outside is better, although you could create an "obstacle course" indoors). The rest of the participants should exactly follow the route taken by the leader. After about one minute, the leader should yell, "switch" and move to the back of the line, causing a new leader to move forward! This can continue until everyone has been a leader or people get tired. The game ends once the group returns to the starting point.

Variations:

- "Injuries" could occur during this activity! Someone could have a broken leg and need to be carried. Someone else might not be able to see and needs to be guided, etc. This adds more challenge to the activity as the group helps everyone navigate.
- Assign leaders by random characteristics. The group might be led by the tallest person, smallest shoe size, nearest birthday, etc.

Fugitive Activity

Time Required:	45-75 minutes
Materials Needed:	One flashlight/Chaser
Activity Level:	Medium-High
Number of Participants:	8-24

This is an exceptionally active and long-term activity done at night. It is imperative that the facilitator put a time limit on how long people will have to complete their quest and achieve their goal! Communication methods (cell. phones) are also a good idea.

The first piece of the activity is to divide a group up into people that are Chasers and people who are "Fugitives". The object for the Fugitives is to get from one location to another as stealthily and sneaky as possible and avoid getting "tagged" (clearly illuminated) by a flashlight of the Chaser. The Chasers must try to tag everyone with the flashlight and prevent them from getting to the final location.

The facilitator(s) will play officials but some other rules need to be in place:

- Safety is important. Do not place locations in traffic or potential areas where there can be harm.
- Determine an appropriate distance between the start location and the ending location. You might go as far as ½ kilometer away depending upon

the group, but probably something in the 200-meter range is more likely.

- Start out with about 10 minutes of preparation and planning time for each side for strategies, etc.
- City locations are OK, but no invasions on private property or breaking of any laws.
- It might be good to inform local police that this activity will be taking place to alert them that people will be sneaking around at night.
- You may wish to set a boundary where the Chasers cannot "camp" or wait for the Fugitives near the end area.
- Chasers must start a set distance away from the starting area as well.
- Give all teams a specific start and end time for the activity. If people are still out at that time, they must end the game and return to the end location immediately.
- You might wish to have a general map of the area that limits boundaries for the exercise.
- Try for a ratio of about 1 Chaser for every 2 Fugitives.
- Other rules as appropriate for the activity.
- Defining what "winning" is for this activity may be important as well. Often the best definition for this is, "Did people have a good time and bond?"

Variations:

- Alter ratio of Chasers and Fugitives to favor one side or the other.
- Make the exercise a "Capture the Flag" activity for the Fugitives. They must get to the end, gather something up and return it to the starting line.
- Instead of flashlights, photos of the people must be taken with cameras or cell. phone cameras.

Get in Line!

Time Required: 1-5 minutes
Materials Needed: None
Activity Level: Low
Number of Participants: 12-200

Explain to participants that this is a non-verbal exercise. The groups will need to get in a specific order depending upon the category that you use. For example, you might ask the group to form a straight line according to their birthdates. People with January 1st birthdays will be at the beginning of the line, July birthdays in the middle and December 31st dates would be the end. There should be no lip-reading or spelling things out with this activity. Once completed, the group can shout out birthdays down the line to verify that everyone was in correct order.

Variations:

- Other ways of getting people in a line could be:
  - Shoe Size
  - True Age
  - Hair Color or Length
  - Height
  - Shirt Color (light to dark)
  - Number of siblings
- Once people are in lines, have them count off in order to form subgroups for other activities.

Group Story

Time Required: 6-12 minutes
Materials Needed: None
Activity Level: Low
Number of Participants: 4-40

This exercise will ask participants to work in teams to create a story. Arrange participants in a circle where everyone can be seen. This story will be started out by the facilitator but continued by the participants. An example of the start of a story could be, "Once upon a time in a land far, far away there lived a vicious troll…" Each participant will then go around the circle (or go by volunteers) and give the next sentence to the story. The next person will provide the subsequent sentence and so on. You can ask that everyone contribute one or more sentences in the circle, depending upon the number of people in the group. There should be a definite beginning, middle, climax and end to the story.

Variations:

- Once the story is finished, everyone will try to repeat the story or act it out in front of the group with participants playing different roles.
- The facilitator can throw in random lines during the story that the group has to react to before continuing on with their story.

I Love You Baby, But I Just Can't Smile

Time Required: 6-12 minutes
Materials Needed: None
Activity Level: Low
Number of Participants: 10-45

Ask the participants to form a circle facing the middle. One person who will start, should approach someone else in the circle and say, "I love you, baby." The player in the circle must respond by saying, "I love you baby, but I just can't smile." If that player smiles while speaking these words, they go into the middle. If the player doesn't smile, the middle person must approach someone else and try again and again until they can make someone smile. No one is allowed to touch anyone else during the activity to try to make someone smile, but anything else is fair play.

Variations:

- You can have the person in the circle alternatively try to make the middle person smile with their response and play the game with a reverse focus.
- Other members of the circle can chime in to try to get the target to smile.

Internet = Me

Time Required: 15-30 minutes
Materials Needed: Computer and/or Internet Access for all to see
Activity Level: Low
Number of Participants: 6-24

This activity is best suited for a large room with a projector and internet access (multimedia room.) Explain to participants that they will be given about 10 minutes to think of one of their favorite internet websites that they will then share with the group. The site can be unique, fringe, exciting (but keep it clean!), popular or any other choice. Once the person finds and shows the site, they have one minute to describe it, why they like it and how it fits in to their lives. Activity continues until everyone has shared.

Variations:

- Focus on humorous websites that each person likes to liven up the mood – not everyone has to share, but this can be a great way to bring levity to a group situation.
- Ask for only websites that are significant to whom that person is today. They should be meaningful and important to each person.

Jar of Fun

Time Required: 15-60 minutes
Materials Needed: Jar, slips of paper, pens
Activity Level: Low
Number of Participants: 6-32

This is a potential on-going activity to use during breaks in trainings or to provide more information about group members. Ask participants to take three slips of paper and to write one thing about themselves that is interesting, odd or unique on each slip of paper. Once everyone has completed this, they should fold the paper twice and put them in the jar.

During the breaks, the facilitator will pull out a slip of paper and read it to the group. Everyone should try to guess who the slip of paper can belong to. Once realized, that person can briefly share the story behind that slip of paper. The person's whose slip it is then draws and reads the next slip and so on.

Variations:

- Participants instead vote on the top three likely people whose slip it is (whether or not is the actual person).
- Points can be earned if people guess names correctly by writing their guesses down.

Machine Game

Time Required: 10-20 minutes
Materials Needed: None
Activity Level: Medium
Number of Participants: 10-120

The object of the exercise is for each group to create a machine using only the people in the group as "material." The facilitator can either have pre-made machines given to each group or can ask each group to create their own machine. Each person must be some part of the machine and either have a motion and/or noise. The group members will then put together the motions and sounds to complete the machine. Each group should have about five minutes to prepare and then present their machine to the rest of the group. The audience should try to guess what the machine is. Examples of machines include: typewriter, washing machines, motorcycles, blenders, toasters, cars, tractors, jet skis, copy machines, cell. phones, UFO, video game units and much more.

Variations:

- If a group creates their own, make-believe, machine. They should explain its function and how it operates – perhaps through a story.
- Each machine has to be mobile and the group must move with it.

Number Groups

Time Required: 3-8 minutes
Materials Needed: None
Activity Level: Low
Number of Participants: 15-300

Participants should have space to move around for this exercise. The facilitator should explain that in this activity, the object is for people to form groups as quickly as possible. The facilitator will call out a number and everyone must work together to get into groups of exactly that number. Those people left over can be "out" for the rest of the activity, or can wait for the next number to participate again.

Variations:

- Have groups do a little math for the activity by getting them in groups of "the square root of 9" or "prime numbers."
- Ask groups to form in groups that are different in quantity than any other group.
- Once in a group, ask participants to do some task or activity before returning to the number group icebreaker.

People To People

Time Required: 10-20 minutes
Materials Needed: None (music if desired)
Activity Level: High
Number of Participants: 12-60

Each participant should find a partner for this activity. Once everyone is paired up, one of the partners should form an outer circle while the other person forms an inner circle. A person without a partner (or the facilitator if equal teams) will be calling out the exercise. Once the caller/facilitator is ready, (or the music begins) the inner circle should rotate in one direction and the outer circle should rotate in the opposite direction. At any point in time, the caller should shout out the names of two body parts (keeping it clean is good – remember where body parts may go). At this point, everyone should move to find their partner and touch those two body parts together. It doesn't matter which person is which body part. The partners who are last to contact each other, as judged by facilitators and people already out, are "out" for the rest of the game. Alternatively, if the caller wishes, they can say, "People to People" instead, which causes everyone (including the people that are out) to get to the middle and find a new partner. The person left without a partner is the new leader, continuing the pairing of the body parts.

Variations:

- Create a new phrase for people to get in groups of 3 or 4 to figure out how to have the body parts connect.
- Don't have partners; just require people in the outer circle and inner circle to pair up. Challenge the group to pair people up by birth month, favorite holidays, etc.

Pinterest

Time Required: 12-20 minutes
Materials Needed: Computer or smart phone access
Activity Level: Low
Number of Participants: 5-18

Pinterest is a website where people can "pin" various things that are of interest to them. These are hobbies, recipes, blogs and other pieces of information.

For those people who don't use Pinterest, they should look at it and determine some things that are of interest via the internet. Otherwise, the activity involves everyone going on the site, examining and then sharing a selection of the things that are of interest to them. They can be related to the group, hobbies, humor or anything else that they would like to share. Participants share until everyone has gone.

Variations:

- If people don't have Pinterest, provide them with magazines, cookbooks or other items to look through and share – either hard copy or online.
- Ask people to share their favorite quotations or sayings from online or other sources.
- Using everyone's list, create a group or team board.

Scare Me Silly

Time Required: 5-15 minutes
Materials Needed: None (blindfolds)
Activity Level: Medium
Number of Participants: 6-25

This activity is meant to get people's adrenaline running. Please be aware that people are healthy enough to handle frights before starting! Also, allow people to "opt out" of the activity if there is a fear of blindfolds or have other sort of trauma in this area.

Get a group of people to spread out in a large area. Ask everyone but one person to get comfortable in an area and explain what will be happening with this activity. One person will sneak up to people and scare those that are blindfolded. Once scared, person removes blindfold to watch the others that will then be frightened in turn. Go around until everyone is done being scared. Also set guidelines about whether touching is appropriate with the activity or not during the scare attempt.

Variations:

- Instead of loud noises, the starting person must sneak up and do some animal noise to provoke laughter instead of fear.
- Anyone who doesn't act frightened can alternatively be the one doing the scaring.

Sing Down

Time Required: 15-30 minutes
Materials Needed: Paper & Pen per team
Activity Level: Low
Number of Participants: 9-200

Participants should be divided up into at least three teams, but not more than six. The facilitator will give the groups a word (i.e. love, dance, boy, etc.) and 3-5 minutes to think of as many songs as they can with that word in the lyrics (not just the title). All songs brainstormed by the group must be written down to be valid. Teams may NOT add additional songs to their list once the brainstorming period has ended. Once the time has passed, one team will begin by having the entire group sing a few seconds of a song from their list with that word in it. NO SONGS CAN BE REPEATED. If a prior group sings a song on your team's list, you must cross it off and you can never use it again. The next team responds with another song and so on. The group that has the most songs at the end wins.

Variations:

- Groups must sing each song instead.
- Give each group a different word.
- Ask teams to bid the number of songs they will create.
- Give each group a musical genre to work with.

Squeeze

Time Required: 10-20 minutes
Materials Needed: An object people can grab (ball, plastic bottle, wad of paper, etc.)
Activity Level: Low
Number of Participants: 12-30

Arrange people into two teams and ask them to sit in parallel lines, front to back with members of their own team. At the front end of the team should be placed the item to be grabbed, equidistant from the teams. (It is also important to have a judge or second facilitator track a mistake or success.) Each team should join one hand with their neighbor and everyone should close their eyes. The facilitator will sit down, grab the free hands on either side of the leaders of both teams at the back of the line and will squeeze them simultaneously at some random point in time. Once that leader feels the squeeze, that person should squeeze the hand of the next person (whose hand they are holding), who will squeeze the next person down and so on. Once the squeeze reaches the person at the front, the first person to grab the object successfully will win that round. The winning team will rotate so that the person who grabbed the item moves to the back of the line and everyone shifts forwards. The winning team overall is the first to successfully get through to their original positions successfully. If a team grabs the item too early, the hand wasn't squeezed by the facilitator or other infraction, the team rotates backwards one person! Note that the facilitator in the back can pause as long as they wish before squeezing or as quickly as they wish.

Variations:

- Instead of a facilitator leading the squeeze, leave it to a game of chance. Flip a coin and squeeze only on a 'heads' or roll a die and odd numbers lead to the squeeze, etc.
- Involve a relay race with the activity and split the teams up. Once it reaches a person at the front, they must do an egg race or some other activity successfully in order to win and rotate forward.

Stackers

Time Required: 8-15 minutes
Materials Needed: Sturdy Chairs
Activity Level: Medium
Number of Participants: 10-40

This activity involves quite a bit of body contact and closeness, so gauge this for your group and audience. Ask participants to start by sitting in a circle relatively close to one another. One person should be designated to start in the middle and be the caller. The caller will make some statement such as, "Everyone who enjoys chocolate, move three chairs to your left." Anyone who enjoys chocolate would then get up and sit down three chairs to the left – even if someone is sitting there. If someone is there, that person sits on their lap. The play will continue with someone in the circle making another statement, people moving and so on. If someone is under someone else when a statement is called that applies to them but not the person sitting on top of them, the entire stack must move. Play continues until people are done. Make sure that chairs are capable of handling multiple people sitting on them or sit on the floor!

Variations:

- Instill a maximum chair limit of three people. Anyone who would be more than that is out of the activity.

Statues

Time Required: 8-15 minutes
Materials Needed: None
Activity Level: Medium
Number of Participants: 6-60

Ask participants to spread out so that there is freedom to move. Explain to everyone that they'll be participating in an activity that will help people relax their minds and bodies. The facilitator will give a title of a statue and everyone will need to physically give their interpretations of the statues and hold that pose for 15 seconds. After those 15 seconds, everyone can relax. This process will continue until everyone has gone through all of the statues. Participants or observers can vote for the best or most creative of each example. The statues to interpret could be (but invent your own if you wish):

- Child at Play
- Anteater with a Full Stomach
- Runner at Starting Line
- Frozen in Fear
- Reflection
- The Dancer
- Cat with Cream
- Happy Dog
- Rubber Band
- Walking the runway as a model
- Zombie Eating Brains
- Pirates Finding Treasure

Variations:

- Instead of the items above, imitate other participants or famous people instead.
- Use cameras to document the statues.
- Ask participants to create their own scenarios in front of the group and everyone must guess what it is.

There's An App for That

Time Required: 15-25 minutes
Materials Needed: Phones
Activity Level: Low
Number of Participants: 6-25

In this activity, participants will share their favorite applications "apps" on their phones or tablet devices. They should share what that app is, why it is their favorite and why it is significant. Sharing should continue until everyone has gone. Should someone not have a smart phone or device, ask them to share a favorite internet website or other item.

Variations:

- Create a favorite "app" list for people that they might wish to download.
- Don't allow any duplication with the app choices. Once someone has said it, it can't be used again.

Think Fast

Time Required: 10-20 minutes
Materials Needed: Random Object
Activity Level: Low
Number of Participants: 8-28

Participants should stand in a circle facing the middle for this exercise. The facilitator will explain that this game will need to be played very quickly. A volunteer will stand in the middle of the circle and close their eyes, keeping them closed throughout their entire time in the center. A person standing in the outer circle is given an object. When the center person says, "Start!" the object is to be passed (not tossed) around the circle to the right from one participant to the next. The center person will then call out, "Stop!" at any time. The center person then will quickly say a letter of the alphabet and the person holding the object must quickly say three nouns that begin with that specified letter. If the participant says three nouns within five seconds, the game continues on immediately, passing the object to the right again. If the person cannot think of three nouns in that amount of time or gets one wrong, they become the person in the center. The facilitator may take the role of "referee" for the nouns to determine whether they are valid or not.

Variations:

- Instead of three nouns, the person selected has ten seconds to say the names of three people in the group with that letter in their names somewhere. If there aren't three names with those letters within the group, then the center person still remains.
- The person in the middle can also say "switch" which causes the passing to switch directions or "toss" which asks them to toss the item gently to someone across the circle and then continue with the passing.

Two Truths and a Lie

Time Required: 8-15 minutes
Materials Needed: None (paper and pen if you wish to write things down)
Activity Level: Low
Number of Participants: 5-40

This is a small group activity, but subgroups can be formed from a larger number of people. The facilitator should ask the group to take about 2-3 minutes to think of and/or write down two things about themselves that are true and one thing that is not - a lie. The truths can be anything that a person has done, something about themselves or about possessions. The lies should be made up but done in the same context as the truths. When complete, each group member will then share all three things about themselves in random order while the rest of the group has to determine which one of the three is the lie. Participants should think of lies that might be believable in order to try and fool the other participants.

Variations:

- Alternatively, people can give two lies and a truth and participants guess which the case is for each person.
- Use themes for the activity - Work-related truths and lies, vacations, childhood, etc.

What I Carry

Time Required: 15-20 minutes
Materials Needed: None
Activity Level: Low
Number of Participants: 8-40 in subgroups

Participants should be split into small groups of three or four. Give them about 10 minutes total (about 2-3 minutes each) to have each person go through their possessions (wallets, purses, bags, keys, rings, tattoos, etc.) explain the items that they possess (those they wish to share) and what they mean. Rotate around until each person has had a chance to go through their items for the group. If participants don't have any items or aren't satisfied with an item, have them describe an item that is in a car or at home that they could share with the group.

Variations:

- Have the participants describe two objects they own that have the most meaning to them. These are the items that they would rush in to safe if there was a fire.
- Ask participants to take one item and put it in a bucket, basket or jar. The facilitator will take one out at a time and either have the owner describe it for the group and what it means or people can pass it around to guess who it belongs to.

Where Were You?

Time Required: 15-25 minutes
Materials Needed: None
Activity Level: Low
Number of Participants: 6-40

Ask people to get comfortable in groups of 6-12 and organize themselves into small circles. As the facilitator, pick a year or a date before the meeting. Once everyone is ready, ask participants to take a couple of minutes to think about and share where they were and what they were doing on that date (Summer of 2007 or January 2003, etc.) with the group. Encourage people to ask questions to try and jog memories as needed. This information can be shared with the large group or broken into smaller groups.

Variations:

- Encourage participants to share what was going on with their lives at that point in time, what was important and what their dreams were.
- Focus on years when participants would be children and ask them at age 12 (for example), what did they want to be when they grew up and why?

Willow In the Wild

Time Required: 10-20 minutes
Materials Needed: None
Activity Level: High
Number of Participants: 7-120

This activity builds and requires a lot of trust due to physical safety. Subgroups should be between about 8-14 or there will be too much space between people for the activity to be done safely. Have a conversation about safety and trust prior to beginning this activity.

Each person should stand close together in a circle with their shoulders touching, facing inwards. Ask for a single volunteer to be in the middle. The person in the middle should have their eyes closed, body, torso and legs stiff and straight, feet firmly planted to one spot on the ground in the middle of the group, and arms folded across their chest. The rest of the group should stay in a tight circle, each person braced with one leg back and one forward with hands up and ready at chest level to catch the person as they fall.

Once everyone is ready, the faller will announce "falling" and the group will respond with "fall away". The person in the middle can fall any direction they wish. The rest of the group will gently catch and change the faller's direction by easing their "fall" and gently pushing them in another direction. After a couple of minutes, switch people in the middle.

Note that the more hands that are on the person in the middle, the safer they will generally feel. Ask participants to remain quiet during the activity for greater impact. Remind participants of the safety involved in this activity and that the key is a gentle push, being particularly careful when pushing across the circle.

Variations:

- Encourage participants to make wind noises or have someone not in the circle fan the person in the middle.
- Ask each person in the outer circle to have a one word affirmation of the middle person ready. Whenever the middle person touches the hands of anyone, that person repeats that affirmation over and over again each time touched.

Zip Zap Boingg Whoosh

Time Required: 6-12 minutes
Materials Needed: None
Activity Level: Low
Number of Participants: 10-35

This activity involves specific motions and rules. It is important that everyone knows the guidelines for the activity. Ask participants to get into a circle. Someone begins by pointing to another person in the circle and saying "Zip!"

That person then points to another person and can either say "Zip" or "Zap." A Zip can be done by anybody who is across from you but not standing next to you. If a person receives a Zip then they can "Boingg" it back to the person who zipped them or Zip to another person in the circle. a Zap can only be given to someone next to you. If somebody gets a Zap they can "Whoosh" it to either person standing next to them. You can only Whoosh when you get a Zap. A Boingg can be done when you get a Zip by somebody.

If someone messes up, delays or gets confused, the round stops and they are out of the game. Play proceeds with the person starting immediately to the right of the person who was out. The game will become more fast-paced as time goes on. This game goes on as long as you wish.

Motions:
Zip – Point with finger at a person.
Zap – Point with entire hand, arm by chest, all fingers extended.
Boingg – Entire arm extended with all fingers extended.
Whoosh – Both arms extended with palms together, pointing in direction desired.

Variations:

- Switch directions with the motions – allowing anyone to point to anyone with any of the motions.
- Allow people to move positions for a few seconds between rounds.
- People may re-enter the game if they can replace members (by tapping on shoulder) that get out.

TEAMBUILDERS

Teambuilders are those activities which build teams, specifically for groups that are long-standing or enduring. These activities often have a message or some piece of education involved. This could be trust, group development, communication, diversity or much more.

Be sure to do some facilitation questions to verify that the group learns from the activity. These are also effective as a part of a larger training session when you want some experiential learning activity.

Remember to have those questions ready in advance and get people to process through effectively!

Autobiography

Time Required: 15-40 minutes
Materials Needed: Pens/Paper (or use next page as a guide)
Activity Level: Low
Number of Participants: 5-35

Give each participant paper (or use the next page) and materials to write with. The facilitator should start the exercise and explain the following scenario to the group: "I am wandering through the library when I notice a book that carries your name on it. It is your autobiography! Being the curious person I am, I turn to page 94 and begin reading." Explain that the exercise is now to write page 94 of their autobiography, with whatever period in time or event that they would choose. There is no "right way" to write the page and any style would work well. After everyone has written their page, participants will come back to the group to read what that page says for each of them.

Variations:

- Instead of an autobiography, it could be a mystery, thriller, sci-fi, romance, etc. with that person as the author.
- If the group knows each other well, then it could be an "unauthorized autobiography" of another person in the group.

Using the space below, write page 94.

Build a Tower

Time Required: 20-35 minutes
Materials Needed: Random items
Activity Level: Low
Number of Participants: 8-50

Divide participants into subgroups and explain that the challenge of this activity is going to be to create a freestanding tower of the greatest height. The groups may use items found in the room, sticks and other outside materials or use materials from a pile that facilitators have gathered. Acceptable materials should be stated or determined by facilitators in advance.

Teams will not be able to brace the tower, use anything other than materials provided and will have approximately 15 minutes to complete their task. Once completed, allow teams to examine each other's towers and process the activity and the communication that took place. There are many variations that this activity can bring, but the processing about roles in the group, how that may change from existing roles and implications team dynamics will be key.

Variations:

- Instead of random items, use straws to create a structured activity for tower building.
- Instead of going for height, try to bridge across some length (2 chairs or tables), and hold the most weight.

- Set up the activity so that one person in each group is an "instigator" who secretly tries to sabotage the group's ideas and presenting other bad ideas. Discussion surrounding trust and teamwork can then ensue.

Collaboration Musical Chairs

Time Required: 10-20 minutes
Materials Needed: Chairs, Music
Activity Level: High
Number of Participants: 8-35

This is a spinoff of the traditional musical chairs activity that many have played since childhood. In this version, no one is eliminated and successively more difficult tasks are placed before the group. People go around the chairs (one less than number of people) to start and when the music stops, everyone must sit down and have no one touching the floor for 3 seconds. Groups are allowed to strategize and talk about how to accomplish this task. Each success will lead to one or more chairs being removed from the circle and the exercise continuing. The game continues until only one chair remains or teams become either too unsafe or are unable to complete the task. Remind groups of safety during this activity and make sure that chairs are of sturdy construction.

Variations:

- Limit the amount of time for the group to succeed.
- Challenge the group to no talking when strategizing how to achieve their task.
- Use a tarp or towel that everyone must stand on instead, shrinking the size of it each time.

Control, You Must Learn Control!

Time Required: 20-30 minutes
Materials Needed: Blindfolds (optional)
Activity Level: Medium
Number of Participants: 10-30

This activity requires everyone to have a partner. That pair of people must then devise their own sound that they will both use to try to communicate with each other. Once every pair has that sound, blindfold each participant in the activity (or mandate closing eyes). Using the "bumpers up" with arms crossed in front of chest, people will safely mill around the room and mix themselves up. Once thoroughly mixed, the facilitator should space people out so there is some space between them. As a group, everyone must try to find their partner, using only the sounds that the pairs created AND without touching any other person in the group. This activity is very challenging and requires communication. If any people touch, then the group must mill around again to mix up and start again. If the group is having too much difficulty, you can opt to make things easier by allowing people to speak words and then alternatively un-blindfolding a participant or two to assist. There is nothing that says a group cannot use OTHER sounds to indicate when people are near. This can also be an exercise in thinking outside the box.

Variations:

- Start with one person directing the people in the activity and then phase them out later on.
- When someone bumps into someone else, instead of leaving the activity, the bumper must sit down and cannot move for the rest of the activity.
- Use multiple rooms nearby for the activity to really spread things out and challenge the group.

Each One, Teach One

Time Required: 25-45 minutes
Materials Needed: None
Activity Level: Low
Number of Participants: 3-25

Ask participants to think of some activity or skill that they possess. The activity can be something as simple as learning how to tie a shoe, telling a joke well, or even making some odd bodily noise. The participants will then be asked to explain and teach it to the rest of the people in the group. The facilitator may wish to provide some lead time prior to the actual activity to give participants a chance to prepare ahead of time. Each participant should be able to go through the process of step-by-step instruction to show others how to complete the task. This exercise works well when taking a complicated task and reducing it down to manageable steps as well as teaching skills at instructing others in a group. The facilitator for this activity may wish to assign a time limit for each presentation of about 3-4 minutes; otherwise people have the tendency to run long. Also, arrange to have everyone rotate through the activity as time allows.

Variations:

- Presenters will be judged by how well the students learn the task.
- Limit the amount of time that presenters have to relay the information.

Facebook & Google Hunter

Time Required: 20-30 minutes
Materials Needed: Access to the internet
Activity Level: Low
Number of Participants: 6-40

This activity utilizes participant's access to the internet via computer or smart phones. The premise is simple, pair up people with someone they preferably don't know very well. Each partner will get the following information about that person:

- Full name
- Hometown and high school name
- University or college name

Once that information is ascertained, give participants a set amount of time to find out what they can about the person via facebook and/or Google. Specifically, you may ask participants to come back with the following:

- Anything interesting from childhood and/or college.
- Make up a story based upon information figured out.
- The most interesting piece of information about the partner on facebook.

Variations:

- Make this an activity where participants have an evening or weekend to do the searching and provide a list of questions that can be answered such as, "Was this person athletic during school?", "Was there a lot on the internet about this person," "What was most surprising about this person," etc.

- Utilize internet at a session to show pictures and links to people that were found.

Five Terms About You

Time Required: 5-15 minutes
Materials Needed: None
Activity Level: Low
Number of Participants: 6-40

This activity is a way for groups who know each other a little bit to provide for affirmations. One person will leave the room while the others that remain will decide on 5 positive terms or adjectives that describe that person. Once decided, the person returns and the group counts to three and says the first term in unison, counts again then gives the second term and so on. Once complete, the next person leaves the room and the process repeats.

Variations:

- Ask each participant to give five adjectives to describe themselves prior to leaving the room and see if there are matches.
- Allow one person to read the five terms instead of the group in unison.
- Mandate one of the terms/adjectives be humorous or silly.

Five Things I Want to Learn

Time Required: 10-20 minutes
Materials Needed: Paper & Pens
Activity Level: Low
Number of Participants: 15-60

Ask participants to take a few minutes to write down five things in life that they want to learn. Then, they should list five things that they are able to teach to the rest of the group. These skills can be professional or personal; tangible or not, depending upon individual preferences. They also don't need to be taught right then and there (e.g. scuba lessons in a classroom). Once complete, the facilitator should ask participants to wander the room and meet people while discussing their lists to determine if there are any matches. Ask people to identify if they also wish to learn or can teach that task for them. This activity works well with larger groups since people are more likely to have matches. Encourage communication within the group in case people don't list something that they wish to teach and learn.

Variations:

- People can sit in a circle and state the things that they wish to learn or can teach, instead of meeting people.
- Use a dry erase board or paper to illustrate the range of things and have people put names by them indicating teaching or learning.

I Am

Time Required: 10-25 minutes
Materials Needed: Paper/Pens
Activity Level: Low
Number of Participants: 8-35

Each participant will need paper and a writing instrument. Ask each person to come up with about 10-15 items that describe themselves, their history, background, family, meaningful moments, interests, etc., and put it into a poem that starts with the words, "I am…" People don't need to be poets to write this piece, but encourage people to not write long narratives, but keep it simple and more in a list-format.

For example, "I am an uncle to three active boys. I am a bulldog drool wiper..." and so on. Everyone will then read their poems to the rest of the group once everyone is ready.

Variations:

- Ask for three different items from different categories to provide more structure to the poetry.
- Provide examples of a haiku, sonnet, free verse, etc., and challenge participants to use these formats.
- Encourage participants to read their poems theatrically with gestures and grand movements.

Information Fun Sheet

Time Required: 30-60 minutes
Materials Needed: Paper & Pens
Activity Level: Low
Number of Participants: 8-35

The facilitator may designate questions for participants prior to the beginning of the activity. Ask the group to answer a series of questions about themselves in an honest fashion. Ask people to write answers on separate sheets of paper. These questions should be able to define themselves and involve at least a moderate amount of self-disclosure.

For example, you may ask people to answer questions such as, "One thing that no one knows about me is…," "The song that represents me the best is…," or "The proudest moment in my life would be…."

Tell participants to not put their names on the question sheets. When everyone has answered, the facilitator can ask the questions out loud so that participants can answer them or even guess who they believe each answer belongs to. The group members can then clarify and explain more things about themselves. Remember that sharing answers in a group setting will also require additional amounts of time.

Variations:

- Alternatively, you may also ask people to type answers for a later session or hang the responses on a wall for people to answer by a set time.
- Ask participants to come up with the questions they would like to have answered as a first part to this activity. The second part would be answering these questions as per the activity.

Perpetual Tag

Time Required:	Up to weeks...
Materials Needed:	None
Activity Level:	Low
Number of Participants:	10-35

This activity is good for an established and long-term group or organization. It is an on-going tag game that can be initiated during a long session or over the course of several days or weeks. The facilitator should privately designate one person as "it" and tell the group that one of them has been told that they are "it." The object of the game is to not be "it." The "it" may tag another person in any way they like (i.e. whisper, text, phone call, facebook, IM, fax, e-mail, mail, through a friend, internet, telegram, message in an envelope delivered by a puppy, chalk on sidewalk, etc.) as long as the person being tagged can realize that they are now it.

The game can last for as long as you wish and can lead to funny stories. The group need not know who "it" is so that the surprise factor is increased and ongoing. There are no rules and no limit to the number of times the "it" can change in any given time period, but there are no "touch-backs" where the "it" goes right back to the previous person.

Variations:

- Alternatively, the exercise could be done where the method of delivering a tag cannot be duplicated while the game goes on – posting a giant centralized poster board (or facebook list or something similar) for all people to see the methods that the tag has been completed.
- Boundaries can be set about when and where the "tagging" can take place. Perhaps tagging during training sessions are off-limits, etc.

Risky

Time Required: 20-40 minutes
Materials Needed: Dice, High / Medium / Low Risk Cards
Activity Level: Low
Number of Participants: 6-24

Before beginning the activity, the facilitator should create a series of questions that people in the group will be asking and answering during the activity. Create about an equal number of low, medium and high-risk questions and separate them into different stacks. Participants will roll the dice to determine which type of card to select from. You may set the results of the dice to be: a 2-6 is a Medium card, 7-9 is a Low card and a 10-12 is a High card. They will read the card and then answer the question for the group. Continue and rotate around the group until most of the cards and questions have been answered. Example questions could include:

- "What is your scariest moment?"
- "What is your biggest fear and why?"
- "Where is the best place you've ever been romantic"
- "What is your favorite ice cream flavor?"
- "What is a secret that no one knows about?"
- "What was your best vacation?"
- "What were you like as a child?"
- "Where is your favorite place to go to be alone?"

- "Beach, Mountain, Lake or City?"
- "Where have you always wanted to travel to, but haven't been to yet?"
- "I feel awkward when other people do...[this]"

Variations:

- Instead of using dice for a random piece, rotate through low, medium and then high selections.
- Use thematic questions to change things up or to get into areas that aren't well known by others – childhood, family, pets, etc.

Self I See, Self You See

Time Required:	30-75 minutes
Materials Needed:	Large Papers and pens
Activity Level:	Low
Number of Participants:	6-40

The facilitator should prepare enough sheets of paper and markers for everyone that participates. Larger groups may require poster board or large sheets of newsprint. Each person will take a minute to write on one side at the top of the paper their name. On the other side, ask participants to write 20 characteristics that they feel describe themselves. Once complete, each person's paper will be passed around (or if large paper and groups, hang the paper on walls throughout the room with tape) and everyone will write comments on the name side of the paper with positive affirmations about what they see! The papers will rotate around until everyone has had a chance to sign them and then the paper is returned to the owner. This is often a great closure activity for a group to use to reflect together.

Variations:

- You can forgo the 20 characteristics and do affirmations to pass around.
- Allow people to add to the 20 characteristics that others see in them.
- Do it as facebook posts.

Shrinking Circle

Time Required: 15-25 minutes
Materials Needed: Rope or twine
Activity Level: High
Number of Participants: 8-30

With rope or twine, mark off one-foot sections and tie the piece into a large circle. The objective of the activity is for the group to manage to fit entirely inside the circle. Once the team has successfully completed that circle, untie the rope and make it smaller with those one-foot increments as a guide. Keep shrinking the rope until the group has determined that they cannot go any further. Remind groups of the importance of safety and not to do anything that is unreasonable or unrealistic.

Variations:

- As an additional test, after the first time, tell the group that they have to figure out how to lift the rope off of the floor and over their heads, but they cannot use their hands.
- Explain that they cannot speak during the activity for an additional challenge.

Tarp Turnover Activity

Time Required: 12-24 minutes
Materials Needed: Large blue tarp
Activity Level: Medium
Number of Participants: 12-35

Spread the blue tarp in the middle of the group with no furniture and a clear space surrounding it. Ask the group to stand on top of it. Once things are ready, explain that the objective for the group is that they all have to remain on the tarp and turn it over completely. Once the group has done that, explain that they now have to fold it in half all while having the entire group remain on top of the tarp. The exercise continues with continual folding of the tarp until the group says they cannot go any further. Remind the group about the importance of safety and that they shouldn't do anything that is unsafe.

Variations:

- Have two tarps about 20 feet apart and explain that they have to figure out how to get the group from one tarp to the other without touching the ground outside of it.
- Ask the group to make specific shapes of the tarp once it reaches a relatively small size.
- Explain that the activity must be done without speaking, or have some people not speak and have their eyes closed.

Touchstones

Time Required: 30-60 minutes
Materials Needed: List of questions
Activity Level: Low
Number of Participants: 14-45

This activity is often best for closure in a group. On the next page, you will find a list of potential questions to ask for this activity. Instruct participants to sit down in a circle facing the outside of the circle. The facilitator will stay in the middle during the entire activity and read off a selected number of statements. The facilitator should explain to the group that everyone in the room has touched the lives of people here in some way. Participants will be called to the middle of the circle and prompted to recognize other members of the group by touching the shoulders of people that fit the specific criteria read by the facilitator. As a facilitator, this activity works if there are about 6-10 separate groups doing the touching or about 3-6 people at one time. Ask participants to count off into subgroups. It is vitally important that all participants remain silent with eyes closed during the activity. People in the middle can touch as many people as they would like, but try to limit it in the interest of time. After the facilitator reads about 5-7 statements from the list, ask the touch-ers to sit down. The facilitator should then call a new group of people to come into the center. The facilitator will then read a different set of statements. The pattern continues until everyone has had a chance to be in the middle. The facilitator should make a point to notice which people are or are not being touched as often and make a point to touch them so that everyone feels "mattered" in the group. It can be disheartening if you are only touched once for 25 different categories! At the end of the activity, ask people to turn around and process the experience. Feel free to create lists more appropriate to your group. Remember to be genuine, emotional and funny – the best questions are a mixture of all three.

1. who fascinates you
2. who would sacrifice for you
3. who you'd like to spend more time with
4. who is a champion for diversity
5. who has (or would) influence you to work on being a better person
6. who has integrity
7. who you hope you don't lose touch with in the future
8. who is (or will be) a great friend
9. who knows how to get things done
10. who you admire
11. who you feel a connection with
12. who is a pleasant surprise to you
13. who you want to get to know better
14. who you feel is a quiet leader
15. who you think is a good listener
16. who really enjoys the role/job they play/do
17. who is quiet
18. who looks out for others in the group
19. who you would go to when you need a lift

20. who has helped you out when you were stressed out
21. who you would want to take a road trip with
22. who you'd like to see speak out more often
23. who you could cry with
24. who loves competition
25. who you think is a future leader
26. who you think is creative
27. who is well-rounded
28. who has even more to offer
29. who you feel is very important to you
30. who works hard behind-the-scenes
31. whose opinion you highly value
32. who you would seek out for advice
33. whose humor you enjoy
34. who you think always has a great attitude
35. you enjoy working with
36. who you feel you could share a secret with
37. who has helped you when you really needed it
38. who has inner strength
39. who is interesting to you
40. who has a positive influence on you
41. who puts in a lot of effort with what they do
42. who works well with diverse individuals
43. who has done something to make you smile
44. who you have shared a good experience with
45. who is very motivational
46. who you would like to share more with

47. who you would like to be more like
48. who makes you feel good about yourself
49. who inspires you
50. who lives an authentic life
51. who is humble
52. who is a mentor but may not know it
53. who is giving
54. who is beautiful inside and out
55. who is great with animals
56. who reminds you of a child sometimes
57. who you want to thank but have not
58. who you have especially enjoyed getting to know
59. who is always in a great mood
60. who would be the best roommate ever
61. who makes you laugh or lift your spirits
62. who can make your heart skip a beat
63. who can tell jokes really well
64. who is brilliant

The examples below are more humorous, but can set the tone for the activity!

1. who you would trade shoes with
2. who would make a good Canadian mountie
3. who looks like hell first thing in the morning
4. who has beautiful ears
5. who is sweet enough to dip in chocolate
6. who would look good driving an old pickup truck and wearing boots
7. who is goofy enough to be a Disney character

8. who would do well if they happened to be in prison
9. who can turn any plant into a dead mess
10. who is often flatulent or gassy
11. who has a funny/silly or really weird laugh
12. who you want to pinch their cheeks because they are just soooo adorable.
13. who secretly has a dirty mind
14. who would make a good hippie
15. who was one of those kids always in the dirt and eating bugs
16. who you could see being in a bad 80's rock band

Variations:

- Participants can only touch three people for each question.
- Ask each person in the middle to select one question to ask and everyone in the middle will respond.

TV Commercial

Time Required: 20-40 minutes
Materials Needed: None
Activity Level: Low
Number of Participants: 5-60

The facilitator should divide participants into groups of no more than six people. Explain that each team will need to develop a 30-second TV commercial that advertises their group (or alternatively some product) to the rest of the world. It should also contain a slogan and visuals that would be effective. Once developed, the team will need to act out the commercial for the rest of the participants (and video it if you can.) Give a set period of time for participants to design their commercial. Discuss some of the various methods of successful commercials (creativity, well-known personalities or actors, humor, comparison to competition, etc.) Process this activity and ask why it was important for the team to work together and how these commercials could even be used in real life.

Variations:

- Ask them to imitate existing commercials or ads, but alter them to fit the group.
- Have an impartial group review the ads for clarity, message and award prizes.

REFERENCES

Tucker, J., *The Ultimate Icebreaker & Teambuilder Guide*, © 2007, Western Oregon University, Lulu.com Press.

The author would like to acknowledge the many different resources available on the topic of icebreakers and teambuilding activities. Many of these activities have been recycled so that the original source is unknown. If you know of the original source material for any of the activities in this guide, please contact the author who will properly reference it in future printings.

ABOUT THE AUTHOR

Jon Tucker is the author of the Ultimate Icebreaker and Teambuilder Guide. He works as the Director of the Werner University Center, Student Leadership and Activities office at Western Oregon University. When he isn't working there, you can often find him with his two English Bulldogs - Owen and Ripley.

www.ingramcontent.com/pod-product-compliance
Ingram Content Group UK Ltd.
Pitfield, Milton Keynes, MK11 3LW, UK
UKHW020221250726
13967UKWH00001B/121

9 781105 928956